NIGH–NO–PLACE

Jen Hadfield lives in Shetland where she works as a poet and writing tutor. Her first collection *Almanacs* (Bloodaxe Books, 2005) was written in Shetland and the Western Isles in 2002 thanks to a bursary from the Scottish Arts Council, and it won an Eric Gregory Award in 2003, which enabled her to work on her second collection, *Nigh-No-Place* (Bloodaxe Books, 2008), in Canada and Shetland. She went on to win the T.S. Eliot Prize for *Nigh-No-Place*, which was also a Poetry Book Society Recommendation as well as being short-listed for the Forward Prize for Best Collection. She has also received a Dewar Award to produce a solo exhibition of Shetland ex-votos in the style of sacred Mexican folk art, incorporating rubrics of very short fiction, and won the Edwin Morgan Poetry Competition in 2012. Her later collections *Byssus* (2014) and *The Stone Age* (2021) are published by Picador.

NIGH-NO-PLACE

Jen Hadfield

BLOODAXE BOOKS

ISBN: 978 1 85224 793 5

First published 2008 by
Bloodaxe Books Ltd,
Eastburn,
South Park,
Hexham,
Northumberland NE46 1BS.

www.bloodaxebooks.com
For further information about Bloodaxe titles
please visit our website and join our mailing list
or write to the above address for a catalogue.

Supported using public funding by
ARTS COUNCIL
ENGLAND

Cover design: Neil Astley & Pamela Robertson-Pearce.

Digital reprint of the 2008 Bloodaxe Books edition..

ACKNOWLEDGEMENTS

Heartfelt thanks to Alex Cluness, Lilias Fraser and Robert, Linda Henderson, Andrew Jackson, Tom Leonard, Klaudia Marosek and James Sinclair who helped me edit *Nigh-No-Place*, and to Janet, John and Marguerite Robertson who made my fifteen months in Canada extraordinary.

My gratitude to the folk of Shetland Arts for their support over the past two years.

And my love to Charles and Bonnie and Natasha Hadfield.

Some of these poems have been previously published in magazines, anthologies and web-journals including *Addicted to Brightness*, *Hudson Bay Post*, *In the Criminal's Cabinet*, *New Shetlander*, *Northwords Now*, Shetland Arts Trust Poetry Postcards, spire poetry poster, and the *Times Literary Supplement*.

'Odysseus and The Sou'wester' was awarded third prize in the Wigtown Poetry Competition, 2007. 'Towhee' won the Robert McLellan Poetry Prize in 2006. 'Thou Shalt Want Want Want' developed out of work commissioned by the BBC.

The last line of 'Our Lady of Isbister' is borrowed from Pen-Ek Ratanaruang's film *Last Life in the Universe* (2003).

This book was written with the help of an Eric Gregory Award received in 2003.

CONTENTS

Nigh–No–Place

I prithee, let me bring thee where crabs grow;
And I with my long nails will dig thee pignuts...
The Tempest

I will meet you at Pity Me Wood.
I will meet you at Up-To-No-Good.

I will meet you at Stank, Shank and Stye.
I will meet you at Blowfly.

I will meet you at Low Spying How.
I will meet you at Salt Pie.

I will meet you at Coppertop.
I will meet you at Scandale Bottom.

I will meet you at Crackpot Moor.
I will meet you at Muker.

I will meet you at Dirty Piece.
I will meet you at Booze, Alberta.

I will meet you at Bloody Vale.
I will meet you at Hunger Hill.

I will bring you to New Invention.
I will bring you to Lucky Seven.

I will bring you from Shivery Man.
I will bring you to The Lion and Lamb.

I will bring you to the North Light.
I will bring you to Quiet-The-Night.

I will bring you to Hush.
I will bring you to Hungry Hushes.

I will bring you to Grace, Alberta.
I will bring you to Nigh-No-Place.

I will meet you at Two O' Clock Creek.
Will you go with me?

THE MANDOLIN OF MAY

Narnia No Moose

*There were stone satyrs, and stone wolves, and bears
and foxes, and cat-a-mountains of stone.*
                    The Lion, the Witch and the Wardrobe

Alberta's a miserable monochrome –
a bootcamp of little brown birds,
no moose,
the grey, grey grass of home.

Canis Minor

He lies in wait like a little headstone
as dry as dry as all Alberta.
I stop to pat his scrubby mohican.
His tongue spools out his head like magma.

Over the Jamieson place
the stars are rising through a peacock dusk
nice and steady in the arid air.

He scours his butt and licks my elbow.
He falls back on his haunches like a telescope,
winking and blinking his sunstung eyes.

Last light. Mosquito bite.
I scrounge a log from the Jamieson woodpile,
an armful of pinecones for kindling.

I put the fire in.
I begin to write this nice poem about your dog.

Dogwalk II

Dervish lilac!

        Local
             lightning!

The tennis ball –
a stale old snottery
coconut, rattled

        and kicked
             on-up the lane.

The fat retrievers,
trawling through puddles!

        Venus-and-a-
             telegraph-pole!

Jupiter,
my baby-rattle!

        Wet claws on tarmac!

White leer of pebbledash!

Still Life with the Very Devil

Nothing in the cupboards
but condiments and liquor;

half a red onion, with parched corona
of carmine and violet, madder and magenta;

a weary
old weiner.

The last clove of garlic spouts a yellow talon.
All I'm good for is a rhyme in *r*.

The sink is plugged with duckstock.
Dishes stacked like vertebra.

Under the broiler,
turned sausages ejaculate.

The Mandolin of May

Twas in the merry month of May,
when the green buds all were swellin...
  Barbry Allen

Big maples and at the end of the lane, the garden bursts
open like a dropped melon. Mealy mash of appletrees, hacked
wet chunk of mountain.

I carry the chamber pot from casita to bathroom. My hems
drag in the wet grass. Cottonseed roils and sinks slowly,
cladding the roof and catching on the gutter like curds.

What the muggy mountain says. 'I beat my breast, thumped
my brother, pulled him to my chest. Roll them down.'

His gold teeth are radiant, a trove of sullen ore; the sweat
runs from his skull to collar. Pouring from the car, the
air-conditioned air curdles.

I'm no great shakes at babies but I've been thinking more
and more about mandolins, as the weeks go by. Crumpled notes
would prang out of those paired strings, a salvage-metal
sound, like freight cars screeling over a crossing.

I'd squash a chord, dent a bumper. Manage a grace note, like
a rock-chip ticking off the windscreen. Notes clip off the
pick like grasshoppers, off a dumped washer-dryer, in the
milky sun, blotted out with wildfire, in Tsiigehchic.

Ping, pang. Every string would have its twin.

If I had a mandolin, I'd hug it to my belly like a watermelon.

A cobweb strains against my shoulder. I cradle the long lens
on a bough.

I step right out into chipping sound, wet daylight and the
river roar. I totter to the river, like a deer or drunken bridegroom.

A slow-worm writhes like a parched old ampersand; a
fisherman cuddles a broad swathe of silver. On every spinner
he lands a salmon – a Chinook – a thirty-pound Springer.

Gravel popping on the drive – a visitor with hopeful eyes, and
a potted daisy in a brown paper bag. Come back at five and you'll
get your bloody hospitality.

My river – warm shallows – rocks and gumbo mud, fish-soup
and dumplings. The glacial rapids – mine, mine like an ice-cream
headache.

Rockhound, I pat hot plutons like favourite nags.

The same spoiled poem over and over; mushy round the
peach-pit of the poem before. The same commas maul it, like
fruitflies.

The famous flood at Elsa's place, when a cedar jacknifed and
tore out a quarter-acre, a Fauve sweep of sand and unanimous
water.

With the white eye of a prophet, the salmon unravels but
swims upriver.

The gabardine mountain pegged up in rain, drooling dye like
a pinafore.

Lock the toolshed, strip the bed in the casita, shake the
clinging seeds, grass, faint hairs from the Hudson Bay blanket.
The fetid, residual warmth of a nest.

I start the last load in the dishwasher and then find the
buttered knife and compost bowl; sagging potatoes; cold handful
of gravy.

Grandmère tonsures a tomato with a sharp little knife. She saws around the withered stalk, excising the sunken socket. On her way to the compost, she offers herself the tomato in her palm, as if she were the horse.

All the way up the lane, tyres lumping over ruts and sinkholes, a robin runs ahead like a pageboy.

Larry's cat is twenty years old and some kinda sage: deep-keeled like a sacred ox, with punka belly and swaying skinny hindquarters.

Grandmère shows which fields are planted with corn. I don't see anything coming.

As she operates the slicer, the girl's butt wags like a hornet's. Bacon accumulates in her palm like insoles.

Grandmère sets down her tumbler. Ice-cubes clank in rye and water. *I thought I heard a bell*, she says. I show the glass, shake it. I said it sounds like the bloody cows coming home.

Kodachrome

Thirty years back, in the Cariboo, Grandmère highstepped the creek, crushing pussywillow to her chest, a bouquet of cagoules.

Your shirt was plaid: red and blue. It *cleared* your belly, thirty years back, in the Cariboo.

Grandmère scooped a firepit with the side of her foot.

You dragged a canoe.

James and Moira ran off for wood. You'd told them to shout – *heybear, heybear* – and did they ever –

Hey bear!

Hey bear!

A godawful wriggly thing fell in Moira's hair.

Moira got a frog in a stranglehold and James, naked, crushed his cowboy hat against his head.

In the sunrise, your plaid shirt practically bled.

Snow still huddled under some of the pines like lambs.

The fields wore cows like fuzzy Hombergs.

Behind, a herd of astounded hills.

The Midnight Visit

Tuilleries of piddle
behind the half-closed
plywood door.

A Bad Day for Icefishing

The tyres creep onto the scab of the lake
and there we are – heh – walking on water.

Smoke-rings clatter from the gas-powered motor.
A wormcast of ice slumps from the augur

and over our fishinghole we bunch like bears,
sift gristly water through a slotted spoon.

We rig the bait – the curled grub and lure –
winch them tenderly down the twinkling fathoms,

stroll them across the wasted lakefloor,
while stealthy, the hole in the ice heals over.

A bad day for fish?
But white noise fogs our lungs and our line.

Your dog makes angels
in the piled banks of snow.

This Is Us Saint's Day

This is us Saint's Day. This is us Saint's Day.
The frescoed snow makes it that way,
the yellow haloes scraped by the tethers –

Benedice.

Bring palms.
Hands to hotly breathing bless.
Pass by Cut Paws and Kennel Cough –
prayer's the run, hell's the kennel –
they coughcough steam,
their agony dwindle.

The sled jerk and the skids crease down hard
and every dog is baying for a six minute run –
broiling bellies in snow, snapping jaws on snow,
drilling pissholes in snow – Deo! Deo!

Hup! Hup! Hup!

Yodelling Gloria as we run, sled-dogs jamp
like strangled surf towards heaven.

Prenatal Polar Bear

He hangs in formaldehyde
like a softmint or astronaut
dreaming in his moonsuit –
a creased, white world.

His paws are opalescent
and dinted with seedclaws –
the flattened, unripe,
strawberries-of-the-snows.

Towhee

The kid in the tree-fort hangs her head,
truant from homework, stuffed tacos, and bed.

The eldritch time: five-thirty-sixish.
She makes the most of loneliness.

She hears her name called across the evening –
Towhee, Towhee, come on in.

They call her name until her name sounds weird.
Towhee, Towhee, a long-tailed bird.

A coyote limps down the railway line.
She whispers the song about Reynardine.

At the fire-hall, they test the klaxon;
she feels the freight approaching the station,

rattling a hundred, poisonous cars.
She sees the accidents waiting to happen.

Tears crystallise in her sweetheart lashes.
Tar boils out of the toffeed sleepers.

The bank drools flame
like a Christmas pudding.

Towhee, Towhee, come in for tea.
She hangs her head like a sacred donkey.

Still Life with Longjohns

Since the longjohns were like bread-pudding,
soggy-bottomed and buttoned
with fake mother-of-pearl;
since I wore 'em on the porch

in the arid, milky morning,
clutching my coffee and looking,
from tight cuffs to baggy middle,
like a manatee, this badlands light

is like the underwear you gave me:
pilled and balding, porridge-white.

Thou Shalt Want Want Want

It is in heaven as it is on thy neighbour's deck –
a plume-tailed cat, a noodle-legged tin table.

You will covet your neighbour's horse
and you will covet your neighbour's land.

You will covet your neighbour,
crawling the apex with a blue tarp in tow.

You will covet bandsaws and braziers,
longbows and throwing knives,

parlour guitars,
shovels snuffling three feet of snow.

You will covet your neighbour,
planting a spittoon for the rain to hawk into.

You will covet your neighbour, hunched over the piano stool
to hammer out the wild, piratical waltzes.

You will covet polkas, quails,
painted pitchforks, a picket fence, a Dutch barn,

a chafing dish, a bain marie,
a kid, a civet, a trivet;

you must have a bodkin, an empire pram.

Thou shalt want want want.
You will covet your neighbour's ass.

Thou shalt covet Warmbloods,
Arabians.

Paternoster

(for A.B.J.)

Paternoster. Paternoster.
Hallowed be dy mane.
Dy kingdom come.
Dy draftwork be done.
Still plough the day
And give out daily bray
Though heart stiffen in the harness.
Then sleep hang harness with bearbells
And trot on bravely into sleep
Where the black and the bay
The sorrel and the grey
And foals and bearded wheat
Are waiting.
It is on earth as it is in heaven.
Drought, wildfire,
Wild asparagus, yellow flowers
On the flowering cactus.
Give our daily wheat, wet
Whiskers in the sonorous bucket.
Knead my heart, hardened daily.
Heal the hoofprint in my heart.
Give us our oats at bedtime
And in the night half-sleeping.
Paternoster. Paternoster.
Hallowed be dy hot mash.

Ladies and Gentlemen This Is a Horse
as Magritte Might Paint Him

Consider this percheron in the climate-
controlled hold, gimped up for the flight
in blinkers and bridle and drugged of course
from the creased Jupiter of his arse
to the spotted dominoes of his teeth,
the burden of his blood alone,
the clapper seized in his brain's bell,
propped up on steel and the air's goodwill.
Ladies and Gentlemen – will you fill your glasses?
May I lead us all in a toast or prayer?
May the horse never wake
that stands in mid-air

the horse never wake that stands in

mid-air

horse never wake that stands in

mid-air

NIGH–NO–PLACE

witless
as the lass who went with Krishna
and beheld in his throat
the complete universe,
I would heft into your lap
my daughter, our *mootie* –
the triangulation point that punctuates infinity;
the diapered Daruma doll, wobbly but equilateral;
cosmic collateral, pyramidal, just *apparently* small;
hair like loose voltage – stray and sparky straw;
grey-eyed, green-eyed, blue-eyed, pie-eyed,
my Macchu Picchu of the Kitchen Floor.
Now, will we visualise
the world? Cell by cell,
Saturn to Sedna, Hells to Valhalla
this and those universes,
aa'

Blashey-wadder

At dusk I walked to the postbox,
and the storm that must've passed you earlier today
skirled long, luminous ropes of hail between my feet
and I crackled in my waterproof
like a roasting rack of lamb.

And across the loch,
the waterfalls blew right up off the cliff
in grand plumes like smoking chimneys.

And on the road,
even the puddles ran uphill.

And across Bracadale,
a gritter, as far as I could tell,
rolled a blinking ball of orange light
ahead of it, like a dungbeetle
that had stolen the sun.

And a circlet of iron was torn from a byre
and bowled across the thrift.

And seven wind-whipped cows
clustered under a bluff.

And in a rockpool,
a punctured football reeled around and around.

And even the dog won't heel since yesterday
when – sniffing North addictedly –
he saw we had it coming –

and I mean more'n wet weak hail
on a bastard wind.

Burra Moonwalk
(for E.M.)

the mumbling wind
the daffodil wheelhouse
the fancy moon
the chapped lower lip
the reestit hocks
a glinder at Foula

the lapwings tumbling
March like a lion
the coarse crumb, Sirius
the Fair Isle bonnet
the horn loopick
the last of the snow

the drowning lace

the sweating windows

the dreeping waashing

the fancy smalls

the asteroidal island

the historical Raeburn

the ducked head

the uncan neighbours

the space wave

the wind-thieved swans

the sieved sunlight

tungsten Sirius

the honeyed windows of home

the wind–thieved smalls

                                 the last of the neighbours

                 the historical quadbikes
                      the daffodil snow

    Foula, like a lamb

                    the reestit sunlight

uncan Sirius

                      the honeyed windows

                    of the homely

              moon

Daed-traa

I go to the rockpool at the slack of the tide
to mind me what my poetry's for.

It has its ventricles, just like us –
pumping brine, like bull's blood, a syrupy flow.

It has its theatre –
hushed and plush.

It has its Little Shop of Horrors.
It has its crossed and dotted monsters.

It has its cross-eyed beetling Lear.
It has its billowing Monroe.

I go to the rockpool at the slack of the tide
to mind me what my poetry's for.

For monks, it has barnacles
to sweep the broth as it flows, with fans,
grooming every cubic millimetre.

It has its ebb, the easy heft of wrack from rock,
like plastered, feverish locks of hair.

It has its *flodd*.
It has its welling god
with puddled, podgy cheeks and jaw.

It has its holy hiccup.

Its minute's silence

> *daed-traa.*

I go to the rockpool at the slack of the tide
to mind me what my poetry's for.

Gish

(for Lise)

Gish, *noun*: a channel of water strained through the wet red grass of a Fair Isle field, where a conger eel, like a swathe of gleaming liquorice, might thresh till nightfall; or, the water that wells in hoof-shaped holes in a pasture; the two rails of faint light in a flooded *gaet* (*footpath, path leading to a beach*); or, a leak from a washing machine; the black liquor that cooks out of mushrooms; or **gish** – if drinking means a person sleeps, the sound of breath like drowning; or **gish** – a pish in the dark, in a severe to moderate wind.

Glid

I turn the camera on my dissolving self,
pale-tongued and rabbit-eyed –

I turn the camera on dazzled
Everything –

plain rain – the loch –
the incandescent horses

forged black against the broch –
me, my brimming head,

precarious as a dandelion clock –
and dimpling the loch,

black button on bright,
a dinghy row-rowed,

skewered with light.

Hüm (noun)

(for Bo)

Twilight, gloaming;
to walk blind
against the wind;

to be abject; lick snot
and rain from the top lip
like a sick calf.

To be blinded by rain
from the north.

To be blinded
by westerly rain.

To walk uphill
into a tarry peatcut
and bluster a deal
with the Trowes.

To cross the bull's field
in the dark.

To pass in the dark
a gate of hollow bars
inside which the wind is broaling.

To pass in the dark
a byre like a rotten walnut.

To not know the gate
till you run up against it.

Snuskit

The shore is just not nice. Good. The hashed basalt is black and all the rubberduckery of the Atlantic is blown up here – a bloated seal and sometimes skull, fishboxes and buoys, a cummer-bund of rotting kelp. The wind topples me, punches me gently into a pool. Beyond, strafed with hail, the sea teems like TV, with frayed aerial. I step back onto my tuffet, boots pooled in buttery light. The wind punches me gently into a pool. I'm doing my best impression of a gull – pesky, pitied, lonely, greedy, hopping up and down on my tuffet. The wind punches me gently into a pool.

Stumba

A transit crawls up on stealthy tyres –
byres bump shore on breakers of fog,
gates pause on hinges of fog,
a cat is crayonned on a throne of fog,
and leaning from the cab in shirt-sleeves,
one elbow rowing the visible air,
it is so mild, he says, as fog
consolidates his stacked, white hair.

Fishing at Spiggie

(for James)

The spinner fluchters,
but falters not
in its bee-line for the shore,

twinkling like space-trash;
beyond, the Djub,
green as ten green bottles, galactic roar.

And you say
It's late for sea-troot,
but we'll hae a few swaps –

God –

we'll put away a few
tonight, bairns – twathree,
three or four.

Self-portrait as a Fortune-telling Miracle Fish

I'm disappointed in the gods that formed me thus
in the likeness of the wall-eyed Halibut;
in my longing, a Meagre or Eelpout;
in my maudlin, a Poor Cod or Bitterling.

I'm disgusted with whichever of you
chose jealousy-with-an-overbite
to be my consort, my symbiotic groupie

and yet some rogue demi-deity
gave a posy of dubious virtues –
made me transparent; electric;

a Wide-eyed Flounder; a Crystal Gobi;
a Stargazer; a Velvet-belly;
a Deepsea Angler, blind,

were it not for this proboscis
that lets me troll my little lantern
in the silt and dim
off the continental shelf.

And my daemon's a dogfish – I think –
a Starry Hound, a blunt and hungry hobo,
scrounging, starveling, sleeping on the go.

Ten-minute break haiku

Just the blades prattling
on cartilage – cut here, here –
a good, fat fillet.

.

My friend the Cuckoo
Wrasse, hauled from his dark holler,
wilting on ice. Alas.

.

Breading haddock, I
bury in the coarse, bright dunes
the pale, wet children.

.

I finger the cur-
ious, quilted sphincter, being
like this, inside, too.

.

Gut-worms, christ! Still I
pluck them from the membranes,
one by one.

Odysseus and the Sou'wester

*When Odysseus and his crew left his island, the King, Aeolus, made him a
final present – a fine breeze for the journey and the leather haversack in
which the rest of the winds were imprisoned, warning him not to let anyone
open the bag. Guess what...*

I caught and oxtered it like a rugby ball,
a bloated bell of beating leather,
and for weeks I nannied the bloody thing –
on my lap, mending sails,
in a papoose, to climb the rigging.
When the boys got steamed on Aeolian wine,
I cuddled my squirming supper of winds –
let no one spell me for a wink of sleep.
From Aeolus to Malea was a waking dream.
Fat kingcups wobbled like boxing gloves.
With open eyes, I dreamt of home.
I clicked my heels in the blinking squill,
pillowed my skull on my second head,
and the boys said
>   *oo*mpa-pa

>   *oo*mpa-pa
>   Rockabye Baby!
as I dandled us home
on the sweet vesper gale.

*

Now the low, brown island strains on tiptoes,
and fences are strung with trembling streamers,
and the sea's mad as milk.

And my cheeks are scored with milky tears.
And like a puffball breaks the bag of winds.

And there's the Sou'wester,
a rising loaf of shuffled feathers,
struggling from the haversack
like a furious swan.

Boreas

She sits the poor old bastard down.
He eats his own parched breath backwards.
The gale doits and diddles in the drains.

Our Lady of Isbister

O send me another last life like this –
I want the same lochans as I had before –
the wind driving spittlestrings
to skimpy shores of dark red stone;
same hot sweet slaw
of muck and shit and trampled straw;
the chimney bubbling transparent heat;
a whirlpool of Muscovey ducks;
paet-reek;
a scrambling clutch of piglet-pups;
the wet socks
slamdunked along the washing line;
the shucked wet shirts in gospel
grey and sparkling sun;
wet white bell
of an XXL tee-shirt,

                            swung

a sheepdog shouting
at my rolling tyres –
polecats, rabbits, caried byres

O send me another last life like this –

This is bliss

                     this

                                    no, this

        no, this

The Wren
(for V.)

This will be your last life here. I see a dropsy helicopter, choring along. A heron like a sickle reaps an Iron-Age sun. I see the Caravan. You've been travelling on your own but – Dear God – like falling face down into warm mud, this is love – the sudden, muddy sun.

You have the Polytunnel. Something about you will need protecting. A bust creel's a debt. You have a debt...doesn't everyone? Money is a pile of anything. Cabbages mean money as manure does. Cool leaves creak between your palms in the evening. It's enough. Pull one.

I see the Wren. Behind and before, above and below you. That's luck. And under the sun, the Dark-Haired Hammerer. In the gleaming grass, the ducks will gleam like curling stones. You'll get off scot-free, trusting everyone.

You will love the land. You will love the land like a bairn. The Hammerer. The Wren. The dropsy helicopter choring along. The heron like a sickle reaps an Iron-Age sun.

Hedgehog, Hamnavoe

Flinching in my hands
this soiled and studded but *good* heart,
which stippling my cupped palms, breathes –

a kidney flinching on a hot griddle,
or very small Hell's Angel, peeled from the verge
of a sweet, slurred morning.

Drunk, I coddle it like a crystal ball,
hellbent the realistic mysteries
should amount to more than guesswork

       and fleas.

Teatros

(Some rockpools for R.)

Jellyfish

Medusae – babes
in the wood, with milky domes
and faint fontanelles;

constellations that
someone shook into the sea,
orphan circlet of

fangs, spasming; a
mussed map of heavens, thimbles
on the tide, all thumbs.

Dénouement

Across the rockpool's frilled theatre,
a limpet budges
a devastating millimetre

Nature Study

Salted tapwater – she knits it
with puzzled antennae;
and from her shell

unpacks a banana bunch of claws,
her googly green haversack of roe,
and last – fascination and woe –

a trailing corkscrew quiff of tail,
a soft nought –
her kernel.

Love's Dog

What I love about love is its diagnosis
What I hate about love is its prognosis

What I hate about love is its me me me
What I love about love is its Eat-me/Drink-me

What I love about love is its petting zoo
What I love about love is its zookeeper – you

What I love about love is its truth serum
What I hate about love is its shrinking potion

What I love about love is its doubloons
What I love about love is its bird-bones

What I hate about love is its boil-wash
What I love about love is its spin-cycle

What I loathe about love is its burnt toast and bonemeal
What I hate about love is its bent cigarette

What I love about love is its pirate
What I hate about love is its sick parrot

SEVEN BURRA POEMS

Burra Grace

I bide on this bit
of broken biscuit –

sodden junket
of peathag, daffodil;

a cramp of basalt
and rosy granite.

I bide on this bit
of broken biscuit

and all its frumpy gods
be thankit:

sobbing wimbrel,
shalder, rabbit,

        peew–t,

     peew–t

peew–t,

peew–t

Nearly a Sonnet

There is no other life
EDWIN MORGAN

If she dies, I simply drown,
but I want to hitch with her a bit;
to point her at the Foula Light,
perched like a mahout on her igneous brow.

THERE IS NO OTHER LIFE.
It is in heaven as it is on earth –
the sodium lamps of Hamnavoe,
the whooping swans' earache echo,

the mild, muddled behemoth, treading water.
And if I drown, I'll go down with her –
lolled in her haybreath, catching her ticks,
dredged by her rubbery cowlicks

of rain, paddling for Canada
in the grim, grey dawn.

Summer Migrants

The blackbird stands on my chimney-pot
and dispenses wetly a song like linctus;

tirricks are back, and the Commander
climbing the road on his two sticks;

and the neighbour I don't know
changes chair to watch him;

and like a hermit crab's, Geordie's paw
sprouts around the swollen door,

followed by Geordie –
come you, come you in.

Bridge End, October

As some attract lightning, and others midges,
I draw behind me a delicate rain –
hooves drumming lightly the steep, dry lane –
a confabulation of wall-eyed gimmers.
Thought of my thought, herd of my heart,
we jink in a flock, in a shoal, we turn.
The school bus – eventual, awful – passes.
The obstacle of a rolling tincan halts us.

No snow fell on Eden

There was no snow in Eden as I remember it.

There was no snow, so no thaw or *tao* as you say;
no snowmelt drooled down the brae,
baring what it should've left kindly hidden.

No yellow ice choked bogbean.
There were no sheepskulls in the midden.

It was no allotment, Eden –
but a hothouse, an orangery,
with maidenhair strummed
by a mumbling monkey.

There was no cabbage-patch of rich, roseate heads.
There was no innuendo and no snow.

No footprint thawed to the sloppy paw of a yeti.

And since in Eden they were so mature,
a steaming bing of new manure was just not funny.

Eve knew no one who was dying.
Adam never sat up late, drinking and crying.

And if at four the sky split like a watermelon,
soddening the land with blue and citrine,
and the drowned ground wept smells,
no one stood stock staring still.

Black was not so sooty, as I remember it.

Green was not so greeny-browny.

No boat twirled redly
on an eyepopping sea.

(if your theory about the chakras is true,
then every blue thing's a voice –
the monologue of cracked tarmac,
the shadow in the lee of each rock
a locket of speech to be broken and heard,
the speaking sky and the speedwell sea,

and in the kitchen, in the night,
sotto voce, the pilot light)

Cabbage

I ask the garden to bear me witness
but what the ground offers me as evening comes
looks most of all like a snoozing face –
whorled, shut, deaf to disgrace –
a mute Om from a drill of Oms,
cool leaves creaking – a Northern lotus.

* * *

Introduction to Economics

The sun is on a spree in town.
It picks things up and puts them down.

At the fleece warehouse, a mated cat says ow
...*wow*...and crawls on its belly to the thick, baled curds

and the blackbirds chuckle and crash like coals
and try to get it on.

The sun spreads my shadow, edible. Ravens broal
and spill their shadows like sump oil.

A guy clears his throat like a speaking horse – broo-hoo!
and this old wife in baby blue bares her teeth, and waves

and I try to make do but
you just can't subsist on light and raw colour, can you?

Can you?

Be they the Adam and Eve
of yellow and blue.

First poem for Owl and Sophie

The sure-to-god-hoax of his footfall
as he burgles his house for the very first time,
his audible paws squishing the carpet,
smacking his lips and sampling the apprehension
around things that should dole out light and heat –
cadaverous boiler, blown grey light-bulb.

And the gale tries to thresh the boons from the house –
the broken gate braced and percolated by darkness,
the onions poked blind in their fishbox of earth,
new cat packed into the crook of my knees –
a drift of scalloped, chilly fur –

so begins a trek of years together,
huddled on the bobsleigh of the blanketed sofa.

In the same way

In the same way she cries at the kitchen door
and I slip her and she runs into circular squalls of rain

and she cries at the kitchen door
with snailtracks of rain in her muscular fur
so I open up and she runs in singing

and she cries at the kitchen door
so I open up and she crouches
then sprints into the wind

and the wind cries at the kitchen door
so I open up and call and call

and she doesn't run in but the wind does,
with rain, a squall of claws –

in the same dogged, idiotic way
I open up, send Goodnight across the brae,

and the wind canters in
and she with a wild carol

and all the night hail
melted gleaming in her furs

NOTES

I am not a Shetland dialect speaker, but the following words flitted through my vocabulary, largely thanks to George William Inkster, James Sinclair and a couple of books – *A to P, an Old Record of Fair Isle Words* and *The Shetland Dictionary* (ed. Graham, The Shetland Times Ltd, Lerwick, 1993).

Some items will be familiar to speakers of Scots.

aa: all, everything.

blashey-wadder: wet and unsettled weather.

broal: cry of a cow or other animal; to cry as in pain.

daed-traa: the slack of the tide.

doit: to be confused in mind.

flodd: the flood tide/the tide coming in.

gimmer: female sheep, between the first and second shearing, and not yet had a lamb.

glid: sunshine between showers.

glinder: to peer through half-shut eyes.

hüm: twilight; gloaming.

ill-tricket: full of mischief and tricks.

loopick: an old worn "horn spoon" used to scrape a pot.

mootie: small; an infant.

reestit: smoke-dried; for example, reestit mutton.

snuskit: in a sulky frame of mind.

spell: to take a turn at work for someone; to relieve...give some body a rest...*I'll gie de a spell.*

swap: to get a "go" at something, a turn.

stumba: a thick mist.

trow: a mischievous fairy.

uncan: strange; unfamiliar; from another area.

Printed in the USA
CPSIA information can be obtained
at www.ICGtesting.com
JSHW081800090924
69561JS00001B/62

9 781852 247935